ETHICAL
DEBATES

Abortio

JACQUI BAILEY

rosen publishing's
rosen
central®

NEW YORK

SAN LEANDRO HIGH

DISCARD

Published in 2012 by The Rosen Publishing Group Inc.

29 East 21st Street, New York, NY 10010

First Edition

Library of Congress Cataloging-in Publication Data

Bailey, Jacqui.
Abortion/Jacqui Bailey.
    p. cm.—(Ethical debates)
Includes bibliographical references and index.
ISBN 978-1-4488-6017-3 (library binding)—ISBN 978-1-4488-7005-9 (pbk.)—
ISBN 978-1-4488-7006-6 (6-pack)
1. Abortion—Moral and ethical aspects. 2. Abortion. I. Title.
HQ767.15.B35 2012
179.7'6—dc23

2011037527

Manufactured in the United States of America

CPSIA Compliance Information: Batch #W12YA. For further information, contact Rosen Publishing, New York, New York, at 1-800-237-9932.

The author and publisher would like to thank the following agencies for allowing these pictures to be reproduced: Cover: Shutterstock Copyright: Vitaliy Hrabar; title page: p10 Shutterstock/Kurhan; p5 Tony Gutierrez/AP/Press Association Images; p6 Shaun Curry /AFP/Getty Images; p7 artwork by sprout.uk.com; p8 Shutterstock/Claus Mikosch; p9 Pierre Guillaud/AFP/Getty Images; p10 Shutterstock/Kurhan; p13 Shutterstock/Perov Stanislav; p14 Per-Anders Pettersson/Getty Images; p16 Brent Stirton/Getty Images; p18 Prashanth Vishwanathan/Bloomberg via Getty Images; p20 Brendan Hoffman/Getty Images; p22, 23 (t) Wikimedia Commons; p23 (b) © Bartek Wrzesniowski/ Alamy; p24 Shutterstock/Benedictus; p25 Shutterstock/Zvonimir Atletic; p26 Wikimedia Commons; p27 Science and Society Picture Library/Science Museum; p28 Library of Congress/Science Photo Library; p30 Shutterstock/Dmitriy Shironosov; p32 Cordelia Molloy/Science Photo Library; p34 Shutterstock/Juriah Mosin; p36 Rex Features; p39 Jasper Juinen/Getty Images; p40 Jay Directo /AFP/Getty Images; p42 Georges Gobet/ AFP/Getty Images; p44 Shutterstock/Vitaliy Hrabar

contents

Real-life case study

This real-life case study highlights some of the issues that surround the debate on abortion.

case study

A controversial case

In 1969, Norma McCorvey discovered she was pregnant and wanted to have an abortion. McCorvey was 22 years old, separated from her husband and already had two daughters, one of whom had been given up for adoption. McCorvey lived in Texas, and at that time abortion was illegal in Texas except in cases of rape or incest, or where pregnancy or birth put a woman's life at risk.

Friends advised her to claim that she had been raped, but as there was no evidence of rape she was unsuccessful. She then attempted to get an illegal abortion but the only clinic she knew of had been closed by the police.

McCorvey was put in touch with two lawyers, Linda Coffee and Sarah Weddington, who were looking for a case they could take to court to challenge the anti-abortion laws in Texas. The case took three years to come to trial, and in the meantime McCorvey went through with her pregnancy and had a third daughter who was also adopted. McCorvey had chosen to use the alias "Jane Roe" for her court case and the lawyer defending the case on behalf of the State of Texas was Henry Wade. The case therefore became known as *Roe v. Wade*.

McCorvey's lawyers argued that the abortion laws in Texas were unconstitutional (against the US Constitution) because they ignored women's constitutional right to privacy — in this case, the right to make a private decision regarding abortion. Eventually the case reached the US Supreme Court and McCorvey won. On January 22, 1973, seven of the nine Supreme Court judges ruling on the case decided that abortion was a fundamental right under the US Constitution. However, the judges also recognized that the government and the states had a duty to protect a pregnant woman's health and "the potentiality of human life" as the pregnancy went along, and they proposed what has become known as the "trimester" system.

This gives women in the US the right to an abortion under any circumstances during the first trimester — the first three months of pregnancy. In the second trimester — the second three months — the ruling allows the government (and individual states) to regulate abortion in ways that "reasonably" relate to "the preservation and protection" of the woman's health, for example, by specifying where abortions can be performed. In the last trimester — the final three months — states can ban abortions altogether if they choose to, except where the life or health of the mother is endangered. This is because at this point the fetus (see page 7) is often capable of surviving outside the mother's womb.

The *Roe v. Wade* decision had a dramatic effect. It made abortion widely available in the US when previously it had been mostly unavailable except illegally, but it also brought about a huge division in public opinion. Since then, those who are against abortion — often known as "pro-life" groups in the US — have fought tirelessly to get the ruling overturned, and many states have found ways of limiting access to abortion. At the same time, those who support legal access to abortion — known as "pro-choice" groups — work to defend the ruling and keep abortion legal.

▼ Twenty years after the case, Norma McCorvey (shown below) became an active Christian and joined the pro-life movement. She now campaigns against abortion in the US, and in 2005 sent a petition to the US Supreme Court asking it to overturn its 1973 decision, but her petition was refused.

Post abortive women say, ABORTION HURTS WOMEN

It's a fact

Worldwide, it is estimated that around 208 million pregnancies take place each year, of which about 31 million (15%) end in miscarriage or fetal death from natural causes, and about 41 million (20%) end in abortion. This means that about one in five pregnant women will have an abortion.

viewpoints

"The [US] states are not free, under the guise of protecting maternal health or potential life, to intimidate women into continuing pregnancies."
Justice Harry Blackmun (Associate Justice in *Roe v. Wade*), *Thornburgh v. American College of Obstetricians and Gynecologists*, US Supreme Court, 1986

"I find nothing in the language or history of the Constitution to support the court's judgment. The court simply fashions and announces a new constitutional right for pregnant mothers and...invests that right with sufficient substance to override most existing state abortion statutes."
Justice Byron White, one of the two dissenting Associate Justices in *Roe v. Wade*, US Supreme Court, 1973.

CHAPTER 1

What is abortion?

An abortion is the ending or termination of a pregnancy before the developing fetus is ready to be born or able to survive. It can happen naturally, when it is known as a spontaneous abortion or a miscarriage. Or it may be done deliberately, when it is known as an induced abortion.

No matter how it happens, an abortion is often a very difficult and emotional event for the pregnant woman. However, a spontaneous abortion takes place because it cannot be avoided, whereas an induced abortion is a matter of choice and so causes an enormous amount of debate and controversy. This book looks at the debate surrounding induced abortions.

The big issues

Is it morally wrong deliberately to end the development of a human fetus, and should access to abortion be limited and controlled by laws? Most people have a definite response one way or the other to both these questions, but of course, it is never that simple. For example, some of those who believe that abortion is wrong may still accept that it can sometimes be necessary. While some who do not think that it is wrong do not necessarily believe that it is always the right thing to do. Both sides might agree that abortion should be controlled by laws, but disagree about what those laws should say.

To understand the arguments over abortion it is useful to know how a human fetus develops in a womb. This is because the question of right or wrong is so closely tied to whether or not the fetus can be said to have a separate life from its mother.

Biologically, a fetus is made up of living cells and so is clearly "alive" in that sense, but while it is in the womb it is completely dependent on the mother for food and oxygen, just like all the other cells of her body. Human life in its fullest sense includes the ability to exist as a separate being, and to be conscious — aware of

▼ Opinions differ as to whether the decision to have an abortion should be left to personal choice, or whether governments should decide on our behalf who can or cannot have one.

one's surroundings and able to think, feel, and respond to them. At each stage of its development, a fetus increases its potential to be a complete human individual, yet as far as we know for certain, it is only able to be one once it has been born.

Stages of development

Pregnancy begins when a female egg cell is fertilized by a male sperm cell and it starts dividing and forming more cells. Over the next 5 to 7 days the fertilized egg slowly moves along the woman's Fallopian tubes towards her uterus or womb (see below).

Weeks 1 to 8

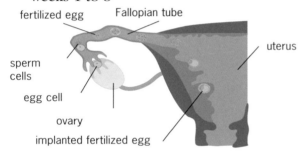

fertilized egg | Fallopian tube

sperm cells

egg cell

ovary

implanted fertilized egg

uterus

The fertilized egg reaches the uterus and implants (attaches) itself to the wall of the womb. At this point it is called an embryo. A bag-like organ called a placenta forms on the wall of the womb and is connected to the embryo by the umbilical cord. The embryo begins developing a spinal cord, muscles, and bones. Cells start to form the major organs, such as the heart and brain. By the end of week 8, the embryo is about 1.2 inches (3 cm) long. It is now called a fetus.

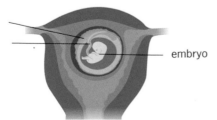

placenta

umbilical cord

embryo

Weeks 9 to 24

The fetus now receives all of its food and oxygen through the umbilical cord and the placenta lining the mother's womb. Small limbs are forming and the fetus makes uncontrolled movements as its muscles develop. Many women start to feel fetal movements from about 16 to 17 weeks onwards. By this stage the fetus has a face, with eyes, ears, nose, and mouth, and all of its major organs. It is approximately 7.8 inches (20 cm) in length.

Weeks 25 to 40

The fetus is growing and putting on weight. Its nervous system and brain are developing the ability to hear sounds and respond to light, and it is continually moving and changing position inside the placenta. After 34 weeks the fetus is said to be viable — this means that if it is born it can survive outside the womb. However, with the use of an incubator and medical help it is possible for a fetus to survive birth from as early as 23 weeks.

It's a fact

Most induced abortions are carried out within the first three months (the first trimester) of pregnancy. For example, according to the Guttmacher Institute (an international research and education institute based in the US), 88% of abortions in the US occurred in the first 12 weeks in 2006. Similarly, statistics published by the Department of Health showed that 90% of abortions in England and Wales in 2008 took place before 13 weeks, with 73% at less than 10 weeks.

What happens during an abortion?

Abortions can be carried out in various ways. It mainly depends on the number of weeks of the pregnancy but there are other factors too. Hospitals and clinics in different countries may prefer to use different methods, or a doctor or patient may choose one method over another because of health or other issues. Abortion laws (see Chapter 2) in different countries may limit the number of weeks at which an abortion can be carried out, or may only allow certain types of abortion — or not allow them at all.

Legal abortions may be either medical or surgical. Both types can have physical side effects, such as nausea, bleeding, and stomach cramps, but many women also experience strong emotional effects too. The decision to have an abortion is not an easy one and although there may be a huge sense of relief once it is over, this can also be combined with feelings of loss, sadness, and depression.

Medical abortion

A medical abortion is brought about by the use of medical drugs (sometimes known as abortifacients). These drugs may also be called the "abortion pill." This method does not usually require a surgical operation or an anaesthetic, although it should always be carried out in a hospital or licensed health clinic.

The abortion pill is safest and most effective when it is taken within the first 7 to 9 weeks. This is known as an early medical abortion (EMA). It can be taken after this time, but from about 12 weeks onwards may require more medical assistance and a stay in the hospital.

The abortion pill consists of two separate drugs taken at different times, either on the same day or a few days apart. Normally the patient can go home after each drug has been taken. The first one is a tablet which is swallowed. This stops the woman's body from producing the hormone that makes the lining of her womb suitable for the implanting embryo.

The second drug may also be swallowed but is more often inserted into the vagina. It breaks down the lining of the womb. Bleeding similar to a heavy period takes place and the lining and embryo are carried out of the vagina with the blood. Side effects can include stomach cramps,

▼ In the days before modern medicine, mixtures made from herbs, such as the common rue shown here, and other plants were widely used as abortifacients.

case study

In 1988, after the abortion pill had been tested in medical trials and was approved for use in France, the French pharmaceutical company that developed the drug mifepristone announced that it would no longer distribute it due to pressure from anti-abortion groups. Although the medical trials had shown that the drug was safe to use, and was simpler and less expensive than surgical methods as it did not require an operation, anti-abortion groups in France and the US were concerned that it would encourage women to have abortions. The groups threatened to boycott the company's other products and held demonstrations outside its headquarters. Two days later the French government ordered the company to remove its restriction. The French Health Minster of the time said the government had made this decision out of concern for public health, and that once the drug had been approved by the government it became "the moral property of women, not just the property of the drug company."

sickness, and diarrhea, but painkillers can be taken. Rarely, and usually illegally, the second drug is used on its own.

Surgical abortions

Surgical abortions involve an operation which must be carried out in an operating theater in a hospital or licensed clinic. The patient is given either a local or a general anaesthetic. A local anaesthetic numbs part of the patient's body but allows her to be awake during the procedure. A general anaesthetic puts the patient to sleep. There are different methods of surgical abortion which can be used, depending on the stage of the pregnancy and other factors as described on page 8.

This photo shows the first of the two drugs used ▶ in the abortion pill, mifepristone, with its developer, Dr. Etienne-Emile Baulieu. After becoming available in France and China in 1988, the abortion pill was then approved for use in Britain and Sweden in the early 1990s, and by the early 2000s was available in the US, much of Europe, and Russia. Pro-life groups in various countries have campaigned against it on both moral and health grounds, although its use is increasing worldwide.

▲ Before an abortion takes place it should always be discussed carefully with a doctor or other health professional, who will carry out a health check, explain what will happen, and talk about possible risks and complications.

Suction method

The most commonly used method of surgical abortion is the vacuum aspiration or suction method, especially within the first 12 weeks. This method uses a thin tube and either a hand-operated pump (MVA) or an electrically-operated pump (EVA) to remove the embryo or fetus and the placenta by suction. The cervix (entrance to the womb) is dilated (stretched open) with an instrument called a speculum, and the tube is passed through the vagina and into the womb. The operation may be carried out under a local or general anaesthetic and generally takes about 10 to 15 minutes. After an hour or two the patient can usually go home.

Later surgical abortions

From about 13 to 24 weeks the surgical method most often used is called dilation and evacuation (D&E). This is similar to the suction method but takes a little longer and is usually carried out under a general anaesthetic. Drugs may be given to help dilate the cervix, and an additional instrument called a forceps may be used as well as a suction tube to remove the fetus. If the abortion is carried out at 20 weeks or more, an injection is given the day before to stop the fetus' heartbeat.

With both methods there may be some bleeding and stomach cramps after the operation and some people can feel dizzy and nauseated after a general anesthetic.

When carried out under proper hospital conditions, a surgical abortion is a safe and fairly straightforward procedure. However, as with any operation, there is always the possibility of complications, such as an infection or damage to the cervix.

Both medical and surgical abortions are usually followed-up by a health examination to make sure that the abortion has been successfully carried out and to give advice on how to avoid unplanned pregnancies in the future.

Unsafe abortions

In some countries safe medical or surgical abortions are unavailable to most women, either because they are very expensive or because they are against the law (see pages 14-15). In this situation, women who do not want to be pregnant are often desperate enough to risk an illegal or unsafe abortion, even though they may suffer painful and severe health problems and even die as a result.

Many women try to abort themselves, using a variety of substances or methods that often do not work and are highly dangerous. These can include drinking

household bleach or turpentine, or "teas" made from herbs, other plants, or even animal manure. Some women try taking various types of drugs, bought or supplied illegally, or they may push something into their womb, such as a sharp stick, knitting needle, or piece of wire to try to dislodge the fetus. Or some may try jumping from a high place, or lifting heavy weights.

Alternatively they go to an unlicensed, either untrained or inadequately trained illegal abortionist who will "operate" on them in a place that is unclean, and who may use illegal drugs or other harmful mixtures, or damaging instruments.

If a first attempt at an abortion fails, women often continue to try other methods, each more extreme than the last and more harmful. And because the attempted abortions are carried out unlawfully and in secret the situation is often made much worse when things go wrong, because the women are afraid of telling anyone, or of going to hospital to get medical help in case they are punished or sent to prison.

It's a fact

According to the Guttmacher Institute, about 41 million abortions take place worldwide each year, of which about 20 million (48 percent) are unsafe. In more economically developed countries nearly all abortions are safe (about 92 percent), whereas in developing countries more than half (55 percent) are unsafe.

summary

► Induced abortion is a procedure for terminating or ending the development of a fetus while it is in the womb.

► Abortions can be carried out in a number of ways, often depending on the stage of development of the fetus.

► When safe abortions are unavailable, women will often put themselves through illegal and unsafe abortions.

CHAPTER 2

The role of law

Women choose to have an abortion for a great many reasons, but mainly because they have become pregnant at a time when they do not want to have a child. This does not mean they do not ever want children, just that having a child at that particular time in their lives is very difficult for them. For example, they may already have as many children as they feel they can properly care for, whether that is physically, emotionally, or financially. They may be single women with no family or partner to help them care for the child, and are unable to care for it themselves because they are too young, too poor, or are not physically or mentally able to do so.

If a woman is young and unmarried, a pregnancy may prevent her from continuing her education or career, or she may fear the anger of her family or the society in which she lives. The pregnancy may have been forced on her by an uncaring husband, or through a crime such as rape or incest. Women are also sometimes pressured into having an abortion against their will, because their family or the man involved insists on it.

Whatever the reason for a woman's decision, how she is then able to carry it out will depend heavily on where she lives and what the law says.

What the law says

All forms of abortion are subject to laws, and every country in the world has its own version. Some have laws that make abortion a crime under any circumstances. Others set limits on when and in what circumstances abortions can legally be carried out. A country's laws often reflect and reinforce its traditional, social, and moral values, and this is particularly true in

case study

Abortion laws around the world

According to a report published by the Guttmacher Institute, nearly one-third of the world's countries have very strict abortion laws. Most of these countries are in the less economically developed parts of the world. Thirty-two of them forbid abortions for any reason at all, while 36 allow it only if the woman's life is at risk. A few also allow it if the pregnancy has been caused by a crime.

Of the rest of the world, 59 countries allow abortion if other aspects of a woman's health are at risk aside from her life; of these 23 include risk to her mental health. Many also allow abortion if the pregnancy is a result of rape, or if the fetus is disabled.

A further 14 countries allow abortion under the same circumstances as above and also include social reasons, such as poverty or the age of the pregnant woman. Fifty-six countries (and territories) do not specify any particular reason for allowing abortion, although they may have other restrictions, such as requiring parental agreement in the case of unmarried teenage pregnancies, or confirmation by two or more doctors that the abortion is necessary.

the case of abortion. However, as with all laws, a country's laws on abortion can change in response to pressure from the public, campaign groups, or institutions, through the decisions judges make when they decide on a particular case, and through changing attitudes in the country as a whole.

Generally the different legal limits or restrictions that are applied to getting an abortion are as follows:

- Not allowed for any reason.
- Allowed if the pregnancy or birth puts the woman's life at risk.
- If it puts her physical health at risk in other ways.
- If it puts her mental health at risk.
- If the pregnancy has been caused by a crime such as rape or incest.

- If the fetus is believed to have a serious physical or mental disability.
- For social reasons, such as poverty or the age of the pregnant woman.
- No restrictions other than the length of the pregnancy.

viewpoints

"In countries with restrictive laws, abortion rates are similar to or greater than those of the rest of the world but virtually all of these abortions are unsafe."
Dr. Kelly Culwell, Senior Abortion Adviser, International Planned Parenthood Federation (IPPF), 2009.

"I think a noble goal for this country is that every child, born and unborn, ought to be protected in law and welcomed into life."
George W. Bush, US Presidential debate in Boston, 2000.

▼ Most of the more economically developed countries, such as Australia, Canada, Japan, the US, and most European countries have fairly liberal (relaxed) laws on abortion. However many also include special conditions that must be met, and in countries such as Australia and the US these conditions often vary from state to state.

Not the same for everyone

Apart from the difference in laws from country to country there is also enormous variety in how those laws are enforced and how easy or difficult it is for a woman to have a safe abortion. Some countries with strict abortion laws, such as Ireland, allow women to travel abroad to have safe abortions although they provide no medical services to help them do so. In others, such as the Philippines, women may be put in prison if they break the law.

In some countries abortion may be legally available but socially unacceptable, often for religious or traditional reasons. Women may have difficulty finding the information they need in order to get an abortion, or they may be prevented from doing so by their husband or family. Also, doctors and other health workers may refuse to carry out abortions because they do not agree with them on moral grounds.

Rich and poor

In developed countries legal abortions may be provided for free as part of a government-funded health system, as in the UK, or paid for by the individual, as is largely the case in the US. Whether it is free or privately paid for, the abortion will be performed by qualified medical staff in a well-equipped, clean, and safe environment.

In less developed countries, the situation is often very different. The country may not have enough clinics, equipment, or trained medical staff to provide a proper service and even legal abortions may be more expensive than many women can afford.

Money makes a difference in countries where abortion is not legally available, too. Women who have money may still be able to buy a professional abortion from a doctor, either in their own country or elsewhere. Women who do not have the money use whatever illegal and unsafe method they can find — often with disastrous consequences for their lives or their health.

The one thing that does appear to be the same everywhere in the world is that abortions happen, whether legal or not.

▼ Young women enjoying a birthday party in Johannesburg, South Africa. In 1996, South Africa relaxed its strict laws on abortion, making them available for any reason up to 13 weeks and for a wide range of circumstances up to 20 weeks. Since the new laws came into effect there has been a large reduction in the number of deaths and injuries due to illegal abortions.

case study

Mexico

The country of Mexico is divided into 32 states and each state is responsible for establishing its own laws. In all states abortion is legal when a woman's pregnancy has been caused by rape, and in all but three when the woman's life is in danger. In about half it is also legal in cases of severe disability of the fetus. However, Mexico is a largely Roman Catholic country (see Chapter 5) and publicly abortion is viewed as socially and morally unacceptable, so in practice, say researchers, it is almost impossible to get a legal abortion. Instead, it is estimated that each year more than 800,000 Mexican women choose to have an illegal and unsafe abortion.

In 2007, the Federal District of Mexico City took the unusual decision to allow abortion on request by any woman up to the first 12 weeks of pregnancy. The abortions are carried out in public hospitals and are free of charge to those who live in Mexico City. If they can afford it, women from other parts of Mexico or elsewhere in Latin America can also obtain a safe abortion in Mexico City, but they must pay a small fee.

In response, anti-abortion groups claimed that the new law was unconstitutional and that the government of Mexico City had overstepped its authority. Also, many doctors working in the city's public hospitals refused to carry out abortions on the grounds of conscience.

In 2008, the law was challenged, but Mexico's Supreme Court confirmed that it was constitutional and the city has continued to make safe abortions available. However, a number of other Mexican states have now changed their state constitutions to make it even harder for women living in those states to get an abortion legally.

It's a fact

According to the World Health Organization (WHO) and the Guttmacher Institute, legally restricting abortion does not in itself make a difference to the number of abortions that take place. In Africa, for example, where abortion is largely illegal, approximately 29 women out of every 1,000 of childbearing age will have an abortion. In Europe, where abortion is generally legally available, the rate is 28 for every 1,000.

summary

► Women choose abortions for a wide variety of reasons.
► The practice of abortion is controlled by laws, which vary from country to country.
► Making abortion legal does not mean that safe abortions are always available.
► When legal abortions are not available, women will often have unsafe, illegal abortions.

CHAPTER 3

Health and welfare

One of the main arguments used in favor of legalizing abortion is the damage caused to women by illegal and unsafe abortions. According to estimates, almost half of all the abortions carried out in the world are unsafe.

Effects of unsafe abortions

In general, those who suffer most from lack of access to safe abortions are young girls and women who come from poor families or who live in poor regions of the world. Most of these girls and women have little education or knowledge of how best to avoid unwanted pregnancy, they often have a low standard of health due to lack of adequate food or health care, and many are already struggling to support themselves, their families, and any children they may already have. In some cases their pregnancy may be due to rape or other forms of enforced sex.

About 5 million women end up in the hospital each year because of complications caused by unsafe abortions, and it is estimated

▼ This charity in Nairobi, Kenya, supports vulnerable young girls and helps them to gain job skills. Kenya has extremely strict abortion laws and more than one third of maternal deaths there are caused by unsafe abortions. Some of them are teenage girls who were raped or who sold sex as a way of helping to support their families.

Each year about 220,000 children around the world lose their mothers because of deaths caused by unsafe abortion. As a result, most of these children end up living in greater poverty than before, suffer increased lack of health and social care, and are less likely to survive into adulthood.

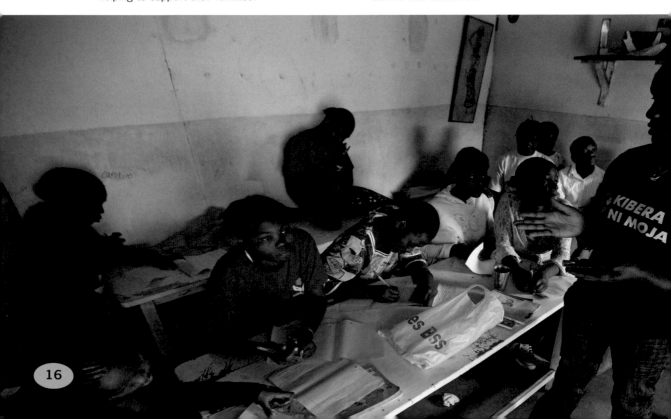

that about 67,000 women die each year from the effects of unsafe abortions (that's about 7 women every hour). Other serious side effects can include long-term health problems and infertility.

Unsafe abortions are costly in other ways as well. Women who are damaged by a botched abortion often end up in the hospital. This puts an added strain on developing countries where hospital provision may already be very limited.

If the abortion is illegal women may delay going to the hospital because they fear that they will be badly treated or reported to the authorities and this can make their injuries worse. They may even not go at all and so suffer severe health problems. In countries where there is little or no free public health care, many women cannot afford to pay for medical treatment after a botched abortion. Instead they put up with painful conditions that leave them unable to work or to support their families.

An unequal risk

Those who are against abortion argue that it is a health risk whether it is done safely or unsafely, and it is true that all medical or surgical procedures carry an element of risk. However, statistics show that when properly carried out by trained medical staff, using modern methods in a clean, hygienic environment, the risks associated with safe abortions are very low, especially when they take place in the first trimester.

It is also true that pregnancy in itself is a risk, both for mother and child. According to the World Health Organization, more than 500,000 women die each year from problems relating to pregnancy or childbirth, including those due to unsafe abortions. Other causes of maternal death

may be severe bleeding, infections, high blood pressure, or obstructed labor due to the size or position of the baby.

Most of these maternal deaths happen in developing countries that are unable to provide much in the way of maternal health care, particularly in some parts of Asia and Africa. The majority of unsafe abortions also take place in developing countries, especially in those countries in which abortion is either banned or heavily restricted. Less than a quarter of developing countries allow wide access to legal abortions as compared to about two-thirds of developed countries.

In developed countries, where most women have access to a good level of health care, less than one in 10,000 die from pregnancy and childbirth, and maternal deaths caused by abortion-related problems are almost non-existent.

viewpoints

"Access to safe, legal abortion is a fundamental right of women, irrespective of where they live. The underlying causes of morbidity and mortality from unsafe abortion today are not blood loss and infection but, rather, apathy and disdain toward women."
"Unsafe abortion: the preventable pandemic," David A Grimes, et al, *The Lancet* Sexual and Reproductive Health Series, 2006

"We always must remember that when a difficult medical situation involves a pregnant woman, there are two patients in need of treatment and care; not merely one. The unborn child's life is just as sacred as the mother's life, and neither life can be preferred over the other."
Rev. Thomas J. Olmsted, Bishop of the Roman Catholic Diocese of Phoenix, Arizona, 2010

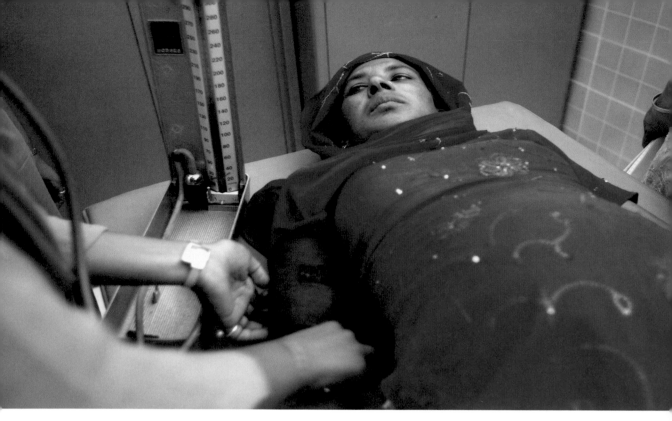

▲ A pregnant woman receives a checkup at a health center in India. Both supporters and opposers of abortion recognize that there is an urgent need for better health care for women in developing countries. Young women are particularly at risk.

Worldwide, nearly 70,000 women between the ages of 15 and 19 die from problems related to pregnancy or childbirth. The risk of maternal death also increases the more times a woman gives birth.

Health options

Those who support the availability of wide legal access to abortion provided by public hospitals and health care centers point to the contrast between the figures for death and injury from abortion in developed countries where it is legally available, compared to those countries where it is not. They argue that making abortion illegal does not stop women from having them (see It's a Fact, page 15). What it does do is make it more difficult and more expensive for women to get an abortion done safely, and makes it much harder for them to get the right kind of medical care afterwards when things go wrong.

Supporters also say that providing access to safe, modern methods of abortion, particularly in the first few months of pregnancy, would help to reduce maternal deaths and injuries. They point out that modern methods of abortion using drugs or the hand-operated vacuum method (see page 10), do not require a lot of expensive equipment and can be carried out by trained staff in small, local health centers, and that this would do a lot to improve the health care of women in poorer areas.

However, supporters also make the case that safe abortion is only one of the health-care options that should be available to women. They point out that the greatest

case study

Legal but not always available

The answer to unsafe abortions is not simply to make them legal. Not all countries that make abortion legally available are able to deliver it safely.

India, for example, legalized abortion as early as 1971, but because of lack of resources and a huge population has been unable to provide a reliable service across the country as a whole. It is estimated that three unsafe abortions still take place to every two safe ones in India.

Because of lack of public health provision many abortion clinics in India operate privately and charge high fees. Where public centers do exist they are often unhygienic and short of equipment and drugs. Most are also found in towns and cities, although 70 percent of Indian women live in country areas.

Social attitudes can also cause difficulties for women in India. For example, it is common for licensed abortion centers to refuse to treat women if they are single, or married but do not yet have any children, and many insist on having a husband's consent, or that of another male family member, even though these restrictions are not required by law.

need is to provide all women and couples with full advice and guidance on all aspects of their family planning and birth control options, including access to all forms of modern contraception, as well as improved maternal health care for women who do want to be pregnant.

A socially acceptable wrong

On the other hand, people who are opposed to abortion worry that making it legally available through family planning and other health centers implies a social acceptance of something that they believe is morally wrong. They fear that this acceptance not only encourages women to choose abortion when they have an unplanned pregnancy, but can put them under pressure to have an abortion when they do not really want one. They say that women may feel that they do not really have a choice, either because they are

single, poor, or would lose their job if they took time off work, or because of the attitude of their partners or families, who may expect them to have an abortion.

Anti-abortionists argue that instead of spending money on providing abortion services more should be done to provide better health care services to help women carry out their pregnancy and to care for any unwanted children that are born. They say that the answer to maternal death and injury from unsafe abortions is not safe abortions, but safer pregnancies. They also argue that if everyone accepted abortion as morally wrong, more would be done to promote motherhood and the right to life of every child, and that more pressure should be put on fathers, families, workplaces, and society as a whole to provide women and children with the emotional and financial support they need.

Preventing pregnancy

No matter what your view on abortion, most people would agree that the best solution is to avoid an unwanted pregnancy in the first place. However, at present there are only so many ways of doing that. Most involve the use of contraception and few are 100 percent successful. Also, women who are forced to have sex against their will often have little or no control over whether or not contraception is used.

In fact, there are only two ways of completely avoiding the risk of pregnancy: abstinence, which means not having sexual intercourse at all, or sterilization, which involves permanently removing or blocking part of a man or woman's reproductive system so they can no longer produce children — and on rare occasions even sterilization has been known to fail.

All other forms of contraception carry the potential for failure — some more than others — and the risk of failure is increased or decreased depending on how carefully the method of contraception is used. The contraceptive pill, for example, is one of the most reliable forms of modern contraception. It is almost 100 percent reliable — but only as long as the woman remembers to take it.

Nevertheless, using contraception does help women avoid pregnancy, and understanding how each type works, which one to choose, and how to best prevent it from failing, is partly what birth control is all about. The other part is accepting what happens when contraception fails or is not used, and a woman is pregnant unintentionally, and that means deciding whether or not to have an abortion.

▼ Members of the anti-abortion movement in the US hold a news conference in Washington in 2009, in which they condemn the killing of Dr. George Tiller. Dr. Tiller ran a health-care clinic for women in Kansas which was known to provide late-term abortions for women who needed them. He had often received threats from pro-life supporters, and in June 2009 he was shot and killed while attending church. The abortion debate can lead to extreme attitudes, and Dr. Tiller is not the only person who has been attacked by those who are opposed to abortion. Clinics have been bombed and other health workers have also been threatened or shot.

Birth control

Attitudes to birth control have changed dramatically in the past hundred years, yet full access to modern methods is still not universally available. Many people who support worldwide access to birth control also support safe abortion as one aspect of birth control, at least within the early stages of pregnancy. They believe it is a necessary part of allowing women to choose how many children they want to have, and is a vital component in improving the health and welfare of women and their families. Aside from the death and injury caused to women by unsafe abortion, having lots of children puts a severe strain on women's health and can push individuals and families into poverty or make their level of poverty much worse.

However, not everyone who supports access to birth control and contraception accepts the need for abortion. Instead they hope that wider availability and better use of contraception, particularly in places where it is unavailable or underused, will reduce the need for abortion.

Others say that using any artificial forms of contraception such as condoms, the pill, or intrauterine devices (IUDs) encourages people to have sexual relationships which they might otherwise not have, and so increases the possibility of unplanned pregnancy and abortion. Some pro-life organizations also say that contraception can lead to an "anti-child mentality," which helps to create a social attitude in which failure of contraception provides an excuse for having an abortion.

A right of conscience

Sometimes doctors, nurses, and other health workers are themselves opposed to abortion on moral grounds, and even though it may be legally available they feel they should not be obliged to carry out an abortion against their principles. In this case they may refuse on the grounds of conscience. Some will also refuse to give women advice or information about how to get an abortion elsewhere.

In the UK, for example, it is generally accepted that a doctor or nurse has the right to refuse to take part in providing an abortion, but they should suggest another doctor or health worker who will help. In the US, some states have laws protecting the right of doctors, health workers, and even pharmacists to refuse both contraception or abortion services on the grounds of conscience.

summary

▶ Unsafe abortions kill and injure thousands of women each year, while safe abortions cause almost no maternal deaths or injuries. Lack of access to safe abortion is hardest on young girls and women who are poor.

▶ Pro-choice supporters argue that making safe abortions widely available reduces death and injury from unsafe abortions.

▶ Those who oppose abortion argue that it creates a situation in which women can feel pressured into having an abortion against their will.

▶ Making contraception and birth control universally available is one way of reducing the need for abortion and for improving the health and welfare of women and families.

CHAPTER 4

In the past

Abortion is not a new dilemma. It has been known about and practiced since ancient times, even though it was always an extremely risky and often very painful process. Long ago, there were no anaesthetics or effective ways of preventing pain, and no understanding of germs or the causes of infection. And although philosophers and scholars from ancient times wrote about the development of the fetus and whether or not it could be said to be "alive," little was known about what really happened inside a woman's body.

One of the earliest written references to abortion that still exists comes from an Egyptian scroll more than 3,500 years old. The Ancient Greeks and Romans also wrote about abortion. Hippocrates, the Greek physician who is said to be the "father" of modern medicine, was against using drugs or other mixtures, but advised women to leap up and down in order to dislodge the fetus and bring about a miscarriage.

Using surgical instruments to carry out operations was known about in the ancient world, but it is unlikely that they would have been used for abortions as the risk of injury or death to the woman would have been high. Instead, the most common method in most parts of the world involved taking herbs or other mixtures — even though these could be equally as deadly. Alternatively, women might try strong massage of the abdomen, lifting weights, or fasting. But no matter what

method was used there was always the danger of chronic pain, damage to the woman's internal organs, or simply bleeding to death.

Herbalists and healers

In the Middle Ages, physicians in the Islamic world included many descriptions in their medical texts of how herbs and other substances could be used as contraceptives, for regulating women's periods, and for inducing an abortion. Few ancient physicians actually performed abortions, however. Throughout much of history, abortion and "curing" women of late periods was mainly the business of herbalists and "healers" who learned their trade by trial and error.

Mixtures containing plants such as hellebore, rue, wild carrot, sage, juniper, pennyroyal, and tansy were widely known. It was vital to get the combination of ingredients right, especially those containing poisonous plants such as hellebore and pennyroyal. Otherwise such mixtures could and probably did kill many of the women who tried them.

This manuscript from the 1200s shows a pregnant woman resting while another woman prepares a mixture for her. The plant she is holding is an abortifacient herb called pennyroyal.

case study

An ancient wonder drug

Silphium is an ancient plant that grew only along one narrow strip of land on the North African coast in Cyrenaica (now Libya). It was used to flavor food and, more importantly, as a medicine. The juice was said to be good for coughs, fever, and aches and pains, the sap could remove warts and other growths, and drinking it helped clean out the womb after childbirth. But above all it was said to be effective for both contraception and abortion. The leaves were made into a tea, and the sap was swallowed with wine or made into a pessary and put inside the vagina.

Silphium was so highly prized that pictures of it were engraved on the coins from Cyrenaica. The Greeks believed the plant was a gift from the god Apollo, and the Romans thought it was "worth its weight in denarii" (the Ancient Roman coin). Attempts were made to grow it, but apparently it could not be farmed. It only grew in the wild, and only in Cyrenaica, and so great was the demand for it that by 100 CE the plant was entirely extinct.

An ancient silver coin showing a stalk of the Silphium plant. ▶

▼ In countries where there is little access to modern health care facilities, many people go to traditional healers like the one shown in this advertisement in Benin, West Africa. Women will often go to traditional healers for abortions, too. In many cases the methods used can cause great physical damage to the woman, or death.

An early form of birth control

In many parts of the ancient world it was generally accepted that abortion was a private matter to be used when necessary, either because the woman was unmarried or had committed adultery, or as a way of limiting the number of children in a family. Reliable forms of contraception did not exist, so aside from abortion the only other way of controlling family size in ancient times was to avoid having sex or to practice infanticide, often by leaving newborns outside to die.

Infanticide as a form of birth control was fairly common in Ancient Greece and Rome. It has also been carried out in almost every other part of the world. At various times throughout history, newborns have been sacrificed to the gods, or killed because they were unhealthy or deformed, the wrong sex (usually female), or illegitimate. Infanticide has also been used in times of crisis, such as famine, overpopulation, or poverty, and even though it is a crime in every society today it still happens.

It's a fact

Infanticide was clearly murder in the eyes of the Christian Church, yet throughout the Middle Ages illegitimate or unwanted babies were regularly abandoned in the streets or left at the doors of churches or monasteries. Known as foundlings, many died. In London in the early 1700s the death rate for children was extremely high. Almost one in four died before the age of five. Some deaths were caused by illness and disease, but many died of poverty or neglect.

▼ Infanticide was such a part of the ancient world it is even woven into its myths. This statue in Italy, for example, represents the story of Romulus and Remus. The story describes how the king of the ancient city of Alba Longa ordered the illegitimate twin sons of a royal priestess to be thrown into the River Tiber to drown. According to myth, the babies were saved and raised by a female wolf and, as adults, founded the city of Rome.

A question of quickening

By 600s CE, Christianity in the form of the Catholic Church had spread throughout Europe and the Mediterranean countries. Early Christian scholars believed that abortion at any stage was murder and a sin. However, in the 400s St. Augustine, a leading member of the early Church, wrote that abortion might be less of a sin if it took place before the fetus gained a soul. He thought this happened at 40 days for males, and 90 days for females.

In the 1200s, the head of the Catholic Church, Pope Innocent III, ruled that the fetus gained a soul when it "quickened" — that is, when a woman could feel the fetus moving in her womb (usually at about 16 to 18 weeks). Before quickening abortion was a serious sin but it was not murder because the fetus was not yet a complete individual. After quickening abortion was murder.

Although different sections of the Christian Church had different views on the validity of quickening, for most of the Middle Ages the law in England and much of Western Europe, and later in North America, generally turned a blind eye to abortion before quickening but made it a crime after that time.

Changing times

By the 1800s, however, opinions had changed. The Roman Catholic Church and other Christian groups had decided that an unborn child received a soul at the moment of conception and so was effectively a full human individual right from the start.

Medical knowledge had also advanced and more was understood about the physical development of the child in the womb.

At the same time, doctors were becoming more skilled and less accepting of the

▲ St. Augustine was a Roman African teacher, philosopher, and Christian bishop. His written works had a huge influence on the early Christian Church.

"untrained" healers and midwives who commonly carried out abortions. They were also concerned about the injuries and deaths these abortions often caused. As a result, laws were passed in Europe, the US, and elsewhere banning abortion altogether, or allowing it only when necessary to save a woman's life.

However, then as now, despite the laws and the teachings of the Church, and even despite the fact that many doctors were trying to prevent injuries to women, abortions continued to happen. Women who felt trapped and terrified by the thought of producing an illegitimate or unwanted child were driven either to attempt an abortion themselves by using a range of traditional "remedies," or to put their lives in the hands of untrained and illegal "back-alley" abortionists.

Pills and potions

In Victorian times abortion was not only illegal, it was regarded as a highly shameful practice and was not openly talked about. Even so, newspapers carried regular advertisements offering all sorts of pills and potions or other forms of relief from "female irregularity" (delayed periods), "obstructions," or other "ailments of the female system." The "cures" they advertised were all various forms of abortifacients and could be ordered through the mail or bought directly from chemists, but were often expensive.

If women could not afford to buy these "cures" they tried homemade remedies passed on from friends or neighbors. These might include swallowing mixtures of herbs, or household chemicals, such as washing soda or turpentine, or even industrial chemicals like lead plaster, or gunpowder mixed with gin. When these failed to work some women would resort to more extreme methods, using knitting needles or other sharp objects on themselves, or if they had the money they would pay an illegal abortionist to help them.

case study

Madame Restell

Madame Restell was probably the most notorious illegal abortionist of her time. Her real name was Ann Lohman and she was the wife of Charles Lohman, a printer who helped publish Robert Dale Owen's book (see page 27). The Lohmans lived in New York City and from about 1839 Ann began advertising and selling birth control products and abortion services under the name "Madame Restell."

Lohman was just one of many people offering similar products at that time, but she was successful and she did not try to hide her new wealth. Polite society was as outraged by her flashy behavior as by her business, and newspapers called her "the wickedest woman in New York." She was arrested several times and even spent some time in prison, but still carried on. Finally, in 1878 Anthony Comstock, the man responsible for the Comstock Law, trapped her into selling him contraception that he said was for his wife. She was arrested again, but committed suicide before her trial.

▲ This illustration from the cover of the February 1878 edition of *The New York Illustrated Times* shows Ann Lohman, or "Madame Restell," being arrested by Anthony Comstock. Lohman was hounded by newspapers and others for her activities as an illegal abortionist.

Abortion was a grave health risk, but then so was childbirth. It was not thought proper to talk about sex and few women knew much about it, or about birth control. To be unmarried and pregnant usually condemned the woman to a life of poverty and shame. But it was not only unmarried women who resorted to abortions. It was common for married women to have several pregnancies, and equally common that they or their newborn babies did not survive. Abortion was sometimes seen as the only alternative to the exhaustion of childbirth and the difficulty in caring for a large family.

People in authority became concerned about the number of abortions taking place. Aside from the deaths and damage they caused, many felt they showed a disturbing lack of morals. Doctors, church leaders, and politicians wrote articles, pamphlets, and books on the physical and moral dangers of abortions and pushed for increasingly harsh laws to deal with them. In place of abortion, they argued that people should exercise more restraint (stop having sex), and that married women should accept motherhood as their duty.

Another solution

Not everyone agreed. A small band of reformers thought that a better solution was to provide married couples with the knowledge of how to use contraception to avoid getting pregnant.

Although contraception was rarely talked or written about except among friends, the most widely used method in the early 1800s was probably coitus interruptus or the withdrawal method (removing the penis from the vagina before releasing sperm). This practice had long been used in Europe and elsewhere, and in 1830 the reformer Robert Dale Owen described its use in the first book on birth control to be published in the US.

Alternatively, women might put a small sponge into their vagina to act as a barrier to sperm, or squirt water into the vagina to wash the sperm out after sex. Condoms for men existed but tended to leak or slip off as they were made of animal gut or fine cloth. Then in the 1860s the first cheap, mass-produced, stretchy rubber condoms became available, along with rubber diaphragms or "caps" that could be used by women in place of sponges.

However, wider access to improved contraceptives led to even greater concern about public morals, and early pioneers of birth control were often heavily criticized and even prosecuted. In the US, for example, the Comstock Law of 1873 made it illegal to advertise or distribute materials that could be used

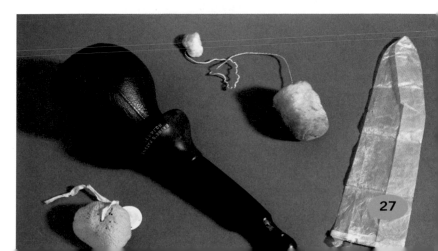

Early types of contraception. From left to right, the picture shows a sponge, a vaginal douche for squirting water into the vagina, a tampon, and a non-rubber condom.

27

for contraception or abortion, or that gave information about them. Similar laws followed in Canada and France.

Nevertheless, the campaign for birth control continued, and by the 1920s a number of social reformers such as Edward Bliss Foote, Emma Goldman, and Margaret Sanger in the US, and Annie Besant, Dora Russell, and Marie Stopes in the UK were writing and giving lectures on birth control. Sanger and Stopes also set up the first birth control clinics for women in their countries.

Most of these early pioneers of birth control promoted contraception as a way of reducing the injuries and deaths caused by illegal abortions. Some were against the use of abortion at all, but

◀ In 1916 Margaret Sanger (right) opened America's first family planning and birth control clinic. The clinic was promptly raided and closed down and Sanger went to prison for 30 days. She continued to write, campaign, and lecture women on the use of birth control until her death in 1966.

case study

The Bourne case

In 1938, Dr. Alec Bourne was a surgeon at St. Mary's Hospital in London. On the 14th of June he performed an abortion on a 14-year-old girl who had been raped by a group of soldiers. Because abortion was illegal, Bourne then gave himself up to the police and was arrested and charged. At his trial, Bourne was acquitted on the grounds that the girl was suicidal and therefore her life was at risk.

As a result of this case it became more acceptable in Britain for abortions to be carried out if the mother's physical or mental health was at risk, and it paved the way for the introduction of the Abortion Act of 1967. In later years Bourne became concerned that the case he had won was responsible for an increasingly relaxed attitude to abortion. In 1967, in opposition to the Abortion Act, he helped to set up the Society for the Protection of Unborn Children (SPUC).

others, in keeping with the growth of the women's rights movement at that time, believed that abortion should be made safer and women should be able to choose how many children to have.

A new mood

Over the next fifty years a great many changes affected people's attitudes to birth control and abortion. In many Western countries, the effects of two World Wars, the growth of industry, and changes in the roles and status of women, made people less willing to be governed by the views of the Establishment — the powerful people and organizations that tend to influence and control social behavior.

Improved methods of contraception became available and the introduction of the contraceptive pill in the 1960s in particular brought about a new wave of sexual openness. Along with other medical improvements surgical abortions also became safer and the manual suction method, already in use in other parts of the world, made its appearance in the US and the UK in the 1960s. Regardless of continuing fears of increased immoral behavior and the collapse of marriage and the family unit, all these improvements were in great demand.

Gradually changes in the law followed, but although acceptance and use of contraception has gained ground in most parts of the world (even if there are many places where it is not easily available), strong opposition to abortion and to some forms of contraception continues.

It's a fact

Although it does not apply to Northern Ireland, the UK Abortion Act of 1967 allows abortion if the physical or mental health of the pregnant woman is at risk, or if there is a substantial risk that the child will be seriously handicapped. Canada began to allow abortions under specific conditions in 1969, as did individual states in Australia. In the US some states began to relax their laws also. In 1973, as a result of the *Roe v. Wade* court case in the US, the Supreme Court declared that abortion should become legal in all states within the first three months of pregnancy, and could be carried out at later stages if a woman's doctor believed it was necessary for her physical or mental health. Between 1973 and 1980, France, West Germany, New Zealand, Italy, and the Netherlands also allowed abortions under certain conditions.

summary

▶ Abortion has been used as a form of birth control throughout human history.

▶ During the Middle Ages, the Christian Church declared abortion a sin because it involved the murder of a human life. However, there was some confusion over when that life could be said to begin.

▶ In the 1800s abortion and contraception were largely illegal, but increasingly used in the Western world.

▶ By the end of the 1900s, social change and medical developments had introduced a new attitude of sexual freedom — although not everyone agreed with it.

CHAPTER 5

A question of life

As scientific and medical skills and knowledge have grown in the past two hundred years, and people's attitudes to sex, relationships, and family life have changed, so the debate over abortion has become fiercer and ever more complicated. But in many respects, most of the arguments that surround abortion come down to a fundamental question, namely:

Should a developing fetus in the womb be regarded as a separate human life, and if so, at what stage?

- Is it from the moment the female egg cell is fertilized?

- Is it when the fertilized egg implants itself into the wall of the womb?

- Is it at some later stage of its development? When the fetus has facial features and begins to look human, for example, or when the fetus is viable.

- Or is it at birth, when the fetus is separated from its mother's body?

The question of life is a crucial one because when people describe a fetus as a "human life" they usually mean more than just alive in a biological sense, they mean life as in a separate human person. Medical science can tell us a great deal about what is happening physically at each stage of a pregnancy, but it cannot answer this question because it is not really a question of science, but of traditional, social, and moral beliefs.

▼ Because of its beliefs (see page 31), the Catholic Church has stated that Catholic doctors or nurses should not have to take part in or give advice on abortions, even if the hospital or clinic in which they work is legally licensed to do so.

Varying views

Some people do not accept that an embryo or a fetus is a separate human person, at least not in the early stages of its development. They say that it is simply a bundle of human cells that is entirely dependent on the mother's body for oxygen and nourishment in the same way as all the other cells in her body. They do not believe that it is capable of individual thought or self-awareness, and medically there is no way to prove otherwise.

Other people say that although a fetus is not a person while it is in the womb it nevertheless has the potential to become a person and so it deserves to be treated with respect. People with this view often feel that the more developed a fetus is, the more it should be considered as a separate being. Many countries reflect this view by setting increasingly tough limits on the stage at which an abortion can be carried out. In addition, there are some people who believe that a fetus is a separate person right from the very start.

Most of the world's religions teach that human life is sacred, and many have a view on whether or not, or at what point a fetus is a human life. However, they do not all have the same view.

The Catholic Church

The opinion of the Roman Catholic Church is very clear — a fetus is a separate life from the moment of fertilization, and to deliberately kill it is murder and a serious moral wrong. Catholics who have an abortion or who help to carry one out may be excommunicated (banned) from the Church, regardless of whether the abortion is legal or illegal in the country in which it is carried out.

The Catholic Church has always believed that abortion is wrong, even though for some hundreds of years it was unsure at what point the fetus gained a soul — a thinking, spiritual awareness of itself. It was once thought that before "ensoulment" abortion might be considered a lesser crime than murder. Since 1886, however, Church law has fully condemned abortion at any stage during pregnancy as the wrongful taking of human life.

case study

In 2009, a doctor in Brazil was excommunicated from the Catholic Church for performing an abortion on a 9-year-old child who had been raped and was pregnant with twins. The child's mother and the rest of the medical team were also excommunicated, although the girl herself was not as she was a minor and in the Church's eyes could not be held responsible. The man who raped the girl was also not excommunicated.

Abortion is illegal in Brazil but is allowed in the case of rape, or if the mother's life is in danger. In this case both of these exceptions applied as the doctor believed the girl was physically too young to give birth without risk to her health. Although Brazil is largely a Catholic country newspapers reported that many people were shocked and dismayed by the attitude of the Church. Some days later Church officials in Rome removed the excommunication.

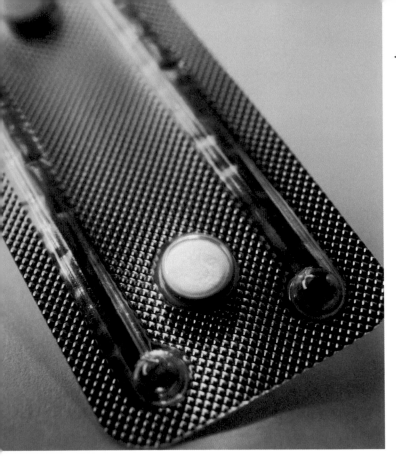

The morning-after pill, or emergency contraception (EC), is a type of contraception that can be taken as soon as possible after unprotected sex to avoid the risk of pregnancy. It is not the same as the abortion pill because it works by preventing an egg cell from being released or fertilized. However, because it is thought that it may also interfere with the implantation of a fertilized egg in the womb it is forbidden by the Catholic Church (along with other forms of contraception). Other religions, such as Islam, allow women to take the morning-after pill, especially if the pregnancy has been caused by rape.

The Catholic Church regards human life as sacred and a gift from God, therefore only God has the right to take it away, no matter what stage that life is at. The Church recognizes that there are situations where the right to life of the fetus or the embryo could conflict with the mother's own right to life, but still believes that this does not give anyone the right to choose one life above another.

As a result, unlike most religions, the Catholic Church allows no exceptions for abortion, not even to save the life of the mother — although it does accept the death of a fetus if it happens indirectly, because the mother requires a life-saving operation.

The Catholic Church does not limit its view just to its own members. It is an active opponent to abortion and often calls on world governments and other organizations to make abortions illegal for all women. It is supported in this by other pro-life groups who are equally anti-abortion although not necessarily Catholic.

It's a fact

Not all fertilized eggs successfully implant into a woman's womb. It is estimated that up to half of all fertilized eggs may be miscarried, in some cases before the woman even realizes that she is pregnant. Yet the loss of these "lives" is not usually recognized in any formal or religious sense.

Other Christians

Most other Christian churches, including the Protestant and Orthodox churches have similar views to the Catholic Church in that they believe that abortion is morally wrong. However, they can vary enormously in the degree to which they may make an allowance depending on the varying circumstances.

The Greek and Russian Orthodox churches, for example, teach that abortion is only acceptable in order to save the mother's life. A number of Protestant churches, on the other hand, would strongly advise a woman not to have an abortion but recognize that it is largely a matter for each individual's conscience.

Islam

Islamic law does not entirely forbid abortion, but does not approve of it either. All schools of Islamic law believe that taking a human life is wrong, but vary in their belief about the point at which a fetus receives a soul and therefore is thought to be a human life. Most think this happens either at 40 days or at 120 days.

Generally, all Islamic schools allow abortion where it is necessary to save the life of the mother, on the basis that this choice is the lesser of two evils. Some will also allow abortion up to the first 90 or 120 days as long as there is good cause, such as if the fetus suffers from a severe physical or mental handicap, or sometimes in cases where the woman has become pregnant because of rape. Others will only allow it up to the first 40 days if there are specific reasons for it, and some groups do not allow it at all.

Hinduism

The Hindu religion is against abortion except where the mother's life is in danger. Hindus believe in reincarnation — that the soul is reborn time and time again until it gains enlightenment and is freed from the cycle of rebirth. Most Hindu scholars think the soul joins with the body at the moment

It's a fact

Some members of the Catholic Church do not entirely agree with their leaders and think that although abortion is morally wrong, there are situations when not having an abortion may bring about a greater wrong. And in spite of the Church's teachings, Catholic women in every country continue to have abortions. For example, one report states that more than a quarter of the women who have an abortion in the US say they are Catholic.

viewpoints

"Any discrimination based on the various stages of life is no more justified than any other discrimination.... In reality, respect for human life is called for from the time that the process of generation begins. From the time that the ovum [egg] is fertilised, a life is begun which is neither that of the father nor of the mother, it is rather the life of a new human being with his own growth."
Declaration on Procured Abortion, given at the Sacred Congregation for the Doctrine of the Faith, the Vatican, Rome, November 1974.

"Of course, abortion, from a Buddhist viewpoint, is an act of killing and is negative, generally speaking. But it depends on the circumstances.... I think abortion should be approved or disapproved according to each circumstance."
Dalai Lama, *New York Times*, November 1993.

of conception and is a fully human person from the very beginning, so if that person is aborted it is deprived of its chance to work towards enlightenment and must wait until it can be reborn again.

Hindus believe that life is sacred and it is wrong to kill any human being. Some teachings say that killing a pregnant women or her fetus is one of the worst crimes possible. However, if there has to be a choice between the life of the fetus or the mother, some Hindu teachings say that the mother should be saved.

Judaism

In the Jewish religion the fetus is not considered to be a full human being until the moment of its birth. However, it is a potential or developing human being, and as such it has the right to be protected and not harmed or destroyed unless there are very good reasons for doing so. Jewish law does not forbid abortions, but neither does it approve of them except in special circumstances. In each case, it is expected that the person or people concerned

would discuss the situation with a qualified rabbi (teacher).

Jewish law states that if the mother's life is at risk the fetus must be aborted, as the mother's life comes before that of the fetus. However, once a child has begun to be born it must be allowed to continue. Most Jewish groups would also allow abortion if the mother's mental health was at risk and it seemed likely that she would commit suicide. They would be less likely to accept other forms of mental distress, except sometimes in the case of rape or incest. Neither would they be likely to give permission in the case of fetal abnormality, although some might if they thought it would lead to severe distress for the mother.

Not right or wrong

In spite of the fact that most religions say that abortion is wrong, many people who belong to religious groups still choose to have them. This implies that when faced with a decision about whether or not to have an abortion, religious belief is only

▼ Buddhism teaches that life should not be deliberately and knowingly destroyed, and that because we are continually reborn life begins at conception. Therefore although Buddhists have no specific ruling against abortion, according to their traditions it is morally wrong. However, Buddhism also teaches personal responsibility and compassion, so many Buddhists accept that abortion may be allowable as long as there are good reasons for it.

one of the things people take into account. They will also think about the effect a child will have on their physical or emotional well-being, They may fear condemnation from their family or society, or that an unwanted child will bring poverty and hardship. Or they may simply have a strong desire not to have a child.

For many people it is possible to accept that abortion is morally wrong yet still believe that it can be necessary in some situations. It is also the case that while many religions may view abortion as a sin, most do not classify it as murder. At the same time, those people who do not believe that abortion is morally wrong do not necessarily think that it is always the right thing to do.

It is also not necessary to be a member of a religious group in order to have a moral viewpoint. Humanists, for example, do not believe in God or any other divine beings, or in reincarnation. Instead they believe that individuals have the right and the responsibility to live their life to the best of their ability, while also respecting the rights and freedoms of others and working towards the common good of all.

This being the case there is no single humanist view on abortion. However, most humanists would probably think that each individual case should be considered separately by the people concerned and all possible options taken into account, and if, at the end of the day, the decision is to have an abortion then it should be provided legally and safely.

case study

Abortion in India

More than 80 percent of the people of India follow the Hindu religion. At the same time, there is a strong traditional preference towards having boy children. Medical science now makes it possible to know the sex of a child before it is born, but usually only in the second trimester of pregnancy, and this has led to a higher than usual rate of late-term abortions of female fetuses in India.

Because of its high birth rate India brought in relatively relaxed abortion laws in 1971, but in 1994 it was made illegal to have an abortion purely on the basis of the sex of the fetus. Currently India has more than 1.18 billion people and about 11 million abortions take place there each year. However, many of them are carried out illegally and in unsafe conditions (see page 19).

summary

► People have different opinions about whether or not a fetus is a separate human life.

► Most religions believe that human life is sacred and the taking of a human life is morally wrong. However, not all religions agree on the extent to which an unborn fetus qualifies as a separate human life.

► Although most religions disapprove of abortion on moral grounds, some accept that there may be situations when it is allowable, at least in the early stages of pregnancy.

► Despite their religious beliefs people may still decide to have an abortion.

► It is not necessary to belong to a religion in order to have a moral view of abortion.

Whose right?

The argument over whether or not a developing fetus exists as a separate person is not only a moral question, it also raises the issue of rights — in particular the idea that people have a right to life that should be protected by law. For example, the Universal Declaration of Human Rights, adopted by the United Nations General Assembly in 1948, states that: "Everyone has the right to life, liberty and security of person." In most countries in the world, this right is upheld by laws.

People who do not accept that a fetus is a separate person argue that it does not have an independent right to life, especially not in the earlier stages of its development. Furthermore, they say that no one other than the mother should have the right to make a decision on behalf of the fetus, and that this includes the right to choose a safe and legally available abortion.

However, many people who have this opinion would also agree that all human beings have a responsibility to respect and value human life, and because a fetus has the potential to become a separate human life, care and consideration should be given to whether or not an abortion is the right choice to make.

Who comes first?

On the other hand, if you believe that a fetus does have the same or similar rights as any other human being, whether or not those rights come into existence at conception or at some later stage in its development, the next question is are those rights more important than those of the mother or less important?

As described earlier, there are situations in which the rights of the mother come into conflict with the possible rights of the

Some people believe that abstinence is the only way to solve the problem of unintended pregnancy. Many Christian, Islamic, and other religious groups ban sex before marriage, and abstinence as a form of contraception is also taught in schools, particularly in the US. The young people shown here belong to an international Christian organization known as the Silver Ring Thing. Each wears a ring to show that they have made a commitment to abstain from sex before marriage.

fetus. It may be that the pregnancy endangers the life of the mother, or was brought about by force and against her wishes, as in the case of rape, or without her full understanding because she was too young, or not mentally able to understand what was happening.

There are other situations that are perhaps less clear cut. For example, imagine a young married couple who do not want to have children yet because both of them need to earn money in order to pay their rent. They used contraception, but it failed and the woman has become pregnant. If she has a baby she will have to give up working, which means they will not be able to pay their rent and will have nowhere to live. They might be able to move in with her parents, but this would mean moving to the other side of the country, and her husband would have to give up his job and may not easily find another.

Should the young woman be able to choose an abortion if she and her husband feel this is the best thing to do? Alternatively, should she be denied this choice in order to give the fetus the right to be born regardless of the difficulties this would bring to its parents?

Rights and responsibilities

Most people would accept that we should be responsible for our actions. If we know that having sexual intercourse might lead to a pregnancy, and that this can still sometimes happen even though we have used contraception, do we then have a responsibility to accept the consequences of that action?

Pro-life campaigners would argue that we do. They say that because the fetus has been brought into being without having any choice in the matter and because it

cannot defend itself, its right to life outweighs the rights of the mother. They say that women should choose to avoid having sexual intercourse unless they are willing to accept the pregnancy that may follow it, or should ensure that they use adequate contraception, knowing that there is a risk that it may fail. Also they point out that if a woman is unwilling or unable to raise a child herself, she can give it up for adoption once it is born.

Motherhood first

Pro-choice supporters argue that the pro-life view puts the prospect of motherhood at the forefront of women's lives, in that it expects them to restrict their emotional and social behavior from the time of puberty until menopause (some 35 or so years) on the basis of whether they do or do not want to have children. They say that the pro-life argument does not adequately take into account the emotional and social development of young, adolescent women, or the commitments women may feel to their husbands or partners. For example, in spite of the fact that the Catholic Church and others teach that couples should only have sex when they are prepared to have children and should abstain, or refrain from sex at other times, in reality this rarely works.

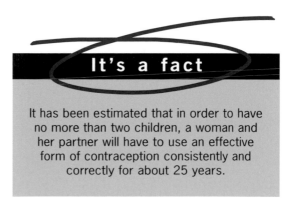

It's a fact

It has been estimated that in order to have no more than two children, a woman and her partner will have to use an effective form of contraception consistently and correctly for about 25 years.

Ability to choose

The anti-abortion view also assumes that all women know about and have access to adequate forms of contraception and are able to choose whether or not to use them. Even in more economically developed countries some women, especially teenagers, may not fully understand the range of contraception available or how to use the different methods correctly. They may not be able to get access to contraception because of parental or family values, or lack of money.

In less economically developed countries the situation is even more difficult. A great many women, especially in poor areas or in the countryside do not know about or cannot afford modern contraception, even if it is available. The use of contraception may not be acceptable in their societies, or they may believe that it is better to use traditional methods, such as the withdrawal method, which are very unreliable. Then, too, many women have no say over whether or when they have sex, but are completely under the control of men, who may or may not bother to use any contraception.

Women's rights

Women's rights campaigners are divided on the issue of abortion. Some argue that one of the fundamental rights of women is the right to control their own bodies and their own lives and that access to abortion, if required, is one of the elements that support this right. However, they would also argue that it is equally important that women have full access to contraception, and, if they choose to have a child, that adequate child care, support, and work opportunities are available to them.

Others argue that providing women with access to abortion allows society to avoid dealing with the issues that lead to unwanted pregnancy. They say that women should be better protected from rape and abuse, and that they should not be put under pressure to choose between motherhood and career or education, or prevented from having a child because of poverty or fear of social disgrace.

Most would also agree that all women should have full access to contraception, although some would suggest that more should be done to focus on male contraception rather than the more

viewpoints

"Forcing a woman to become a mother against her wishes comes from the same place as banning her from opening a bank account in her name or excluding her from the right to vote."
Irina Lester, "Abortion: Still a Feminist Issue," article in the online magazine, *The F-Word*

"... abortion is a symptom of, not a solution to, the continuing struggles women face in the workplace, at home and in society."
Serrin M. Foster, President, Feminists for Life, 1999.

It's a fact

Research carried out by the Guttmacher Institute for the United Nations Population Fund has estimated that more than 200 million women wanted but were unable to get modern contraceptives, and that about two-thirds of all unintended pregnancies were the result of not using contraceptives. In 2008, it was estimated that 75 million women became pregnant when they did not intend to.

complicated or invasive methods, such as the pill or the IUD, that are currently promoted for women and which can have unwanted side effects. They might also argue against abortion on the grounds that it allows men to exploit women sexually without having to take responsibility for the children that result, or alternatively undergo a potentially dangerous operation.

What about the father?

Most of the debate about abortion revolves around the rights of the fetus and the mother, but what rights and responsibilities does the father have? In most societies a man is generally expected to take some share in the responsibility for avoiding an unplanned or unwanted pregnancy, and certainly condoms are far cheaper and more readily available than most other forms of contraception.

It is also usually assumed that men have a moral obligation to accept responsibility for any child that they father, regardless of whether or not they are married to the mother, even if it is only to provide financial support.

However, it is often (though not always) the case that when there is no ongoing relationship between the mother and father the man's involvement, if any, quickly falls away. Because of this it is widely recognized that as well as carrying the physical burden of pregnancy, it is usually women who bear the major responsibility for bringing up any children they have. Therefore it is the woman's physical, emotional, and social state rather than the man's that is of most concern when the question of abortion arises.

When couples are in a close relationship they usually make a decision over an unplanned pregnancy together. However, in most Western societies men do not have any legal right to either prevent or insist on an abortion regardless of their relationship to the mother. In some other parts of the world, though, a husband may have both a traditional and a legal right to prevent a wife from having an abortion if he does not want her to.

A number of men are anti-abortion activists, like those shown here in this pro-life demonstration in Spain. In the last 30 years, there have been a few cases in both the UK and the US of men taking a woman to court in an attempt to prevent her having an abortion, often with the support of pro-life organizations. To date, no such cases have been won.

39

Life under any circumstances

Another aspect that arises from the belief that an unborn child has the right to life is an assumption that it would choose life no matter what kind of life that may be. For example, if a fetus is so badly deformed that it will be unable to live a normal life after it is born does it have a right not to be born? Obviously the fetus cannot make this decision for itself and so the parents must decide on its behalf.

Some people say that along with a right to life comes an obligation to life and no one, not even the individual concerned, has a right to deliberately end that life for any reason. This is an argument that most often comes up in the debate around euthanasia (voluntarily ending one's life when suffering from an incurable disease). Others view quality of life as a vital part of life itself and take into consideration the likely future of the child once it is born.

▼ Homeless children sleep on a street in Manila in the Philippines. The Philippines is a mainly Catholic country and the Church has put pressure on the government there to restrict access to birth control. As a result, one in three newborns are unwanted or unplanned. No one knows exactly how many street children there are in the world, but estimates put the number at about 100 million. Some are there because their families have nowhere else to live, but many do not have families, either because their parents have died or have been separated from them by war or natural disaster, or because they have been abandoned.

What are the alternatives?

Women who find themselves pregnant when they do not wish to be have a limited number of options, and the choice they make will be heavily influenced by their personal situation and their emotional response. An unplanned pregnancy can make a woman feel frightened, trapped and panicky, and desperately unhappy.

She can go ahead with the pregnancy and keep the child, but if she does not have a partner or family to support her she will have to depend entirely on her own ability to earn money at the same time as caring for the baby, or rely on government-funded or charitable support, if it is available. If she does have a partner or family their ability to support a child will depend on where they live, how many other children they already have, and how rich or poor they are. If the mother is young and still at school or college she will probably have to give up her studies and will most likely lose many of her friends and her social life.

If she decides to go ahead with the pregnancy but cannot care for the child herself she may be able to give it to an agency that will arrange for it to be adopted by someone else. However, this is often a heartbreaking choice to make after going through nine months of pregnancy and a birth, and there is no guarantee that the baby will find a loving home.

In fact, depending on where the mother lives there may not be an organization that is able to find a family to adopt the child. It may grow up entirely in an orphanage or some other charitable institution. Or, if there are no institutions to care for it the child might end up homeless and abandoned, even though abandoning a child, especially a newborn, is a crime in most countries.

If, however, a woman chooses to have an abortion she will usually feel enormous sadness and guilt even if she is sure that it is the right choice for her.

case study

Disability rights

Some disabled people argue that laws that specifically allow abortion on the grounds of disability discriminate against disabled people because they imply that disabled people are less "normal" and therefore of less value than other people. They say that it is no more acceptable to allow abortion purely on the grounds of disability than it would be on the grounds of gender, race, or physical features. In addition, they say that most of the problems disabled people face in their ability to live a normal life have more to do with social prejudice than anything else, and that all fetuses should be regarded equally in law.

It's a fact

Research carried out in the US showed that making abortion legal in the early 1970s reduced the number of children put up for adoption.

Romania

In 1957, Romania made abortion legally available on demand within the first 14 weeks of pregnancy. In 1966, after a change in government, abortion and contraception were severely restricted in an effort to force women to have more children to counteract the country's fall in population. At first this was successful, but eventually the number of births fell again as the rate of illegal abortions rose. By 1989, deaths due to unsafe abortions accounted for more than 80 percent of all maternal deaths. It is also estimated that up to 20 percent of women became infertile due to repeated abortions — some having as many as five illegal abortions by the age of 40. At the same time, increasing numbers of children had been abandoned and taken into crowded and unsanitary orphanages where many died.

After the revolution in Romania in 1989, abortion was legalized again. In the first year the abortion rate rose sharply, but has fallen steadily since then. At the same time, maternal deaths have fallen by nearly two-thirds.

Population control

People's right to plan and control their own reproduction, including the right to choose or not to choose to have an abortion, is also an issue that comes up in relation to the world's population. In the last 200 years, the number of people in the world has increased from 1 billion in 1804 to 6.7 billion in 2010, and as far as anyone can tell it will carry on rising until at least 2050.

Some people believe that there is a limit to how many of us the planet can support, and that eventually we will run out of food, fresh water, and land on which to live. When this happens they fear there will be even more poverty, famine, pollution, and war as we start to run out of resources. They argue that free access to safe abortions is one way that governments can help to control population growth.

▼ A young mother visits a health center in Liberia, Africa. In 1994, the UN International Conference on Population and Development called for worldwide access to sexual and reproductive health care by 2015, including family planning, maternal, and infant health care. However, there are still countries where many people do not have these services, either because their governments do not have the money to provide them, or because they do not want to provide them.

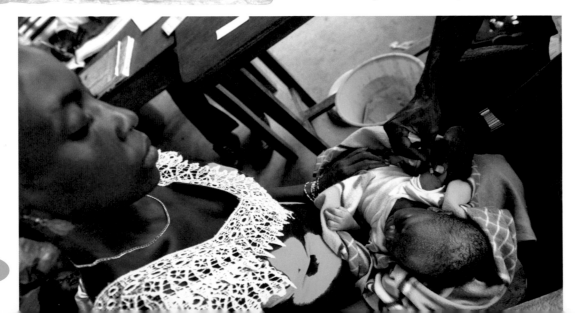

case study

China

China has the biggest population in the world (1.3 billion). It began its One-Child Policy in 1979. This officially forbids married couples to have more than one child, although it does make some allowances for minority groups, people that live in the countryside, and couples who have no brothers and sisters. The policy is policed on a local level and varies from region to region. Married women must obtain a license to have a child, and couples who have more children without permission pay a large fine and pay for education and health care. After a first or second child many women are sterilized, sometimes against their will. Unmarried women are not expected to get pregnant, so although contraception is freely available in China many unmarried women do not use it and will often have an abortion if they become pregnant.

Although the policy has been successful in reducing China's population growth and, according to the government, has helped to improve people's access to jobs, health care, education, and housing overall, the population is still increasing and the government has been criticized for the way in which the policy is enforced. In spite of the fact that it is against the law, there have been examples of government officials making women have abortions even at a late stage in pregnancy.

In response, other groups argue that the answer is not to limit the number of children people have, but to make sure that the world's supplies of food, fresh water, and wealth are more fairly shared out between the developed and the developing countries.

Many also fear that when governments get involved in population control they can bring unfair pressure on people in an effort to force them to stop having children, or even, in some cases, to have more children than they want — as the two examples given here show.

In either case they argue that no government or other organization should interfere with people's right to choose for themselves how many children to have and when to have them.

summary

▶ People who believe that a fetus is a separate human life argue that this gives it a basic right to life.

▶ Some believe the right to life of the fetus comes before the rights of the mother. Others disagree and say that women's rights and needs regarding their own lives come first.

▶ Some people believe the fetus has a right to life regardless of what its circumstances may be when it is born. Others argue that its future quality of life should also be taken into account.

▶ Government policies that deal with birth rates and population control can be used in ways that infringe people's human rights.

CHAPTER 7

A continuing debate

It is likely that the debate on abortion will continue for as long as there are people to have it — and it is probably right that it should. Abortion deals with fundamental principles concerning human life — what it is, the value we place on it, what rights we have as human beings, and what our responsibilities are, both to ourselves and to others — and we should not take such principles for granted.

Those who believe that an unborn child has an absolute right to life from the moment of conception are not likely to be persuaded otherwise by arguments based on the mother's right to health or relief from poverty, or even the right not to be forced into doing something .

Equally, those who believe that the mother's needs outweigh all others are not going to accept that women should not have the right to decide for themselves whether or not to have an abortion. Remember, the pro-choice argument is

not necessarily saying that abortion is a good thing, it is accepting that abortion may sometimes be a necessary thing, and that women must have freedom of choice.

Between these two ends of the spectrum is a vast range of opinions, involving issues such as timing, methods, and the health and viability of the mother and the fetus.

Informed choice

Ultimately, perhaps, the balance lies in creating a society that accepts that individuals have the right and the responsibility for making their own decisions when it comes to abortion, and makes sure that each is given the information and support to make those decisions. In such a society, abortion would be a choice of last resort, and the aim would always be to avoid unwanted pregnancies in the first place.

One good example of how this can work is the Netherlands, which has one of the

Supporters of sex education in schools believe that it is the only way to help young people to avoid unintended pregnancy and the possibility of an abortion. Opposers say that it encourages young people to take part in risky sexual behavior. Research tends to show that comprehensive and consistent sex education can be effective in reducing teenage pregnancy. ▶

lowest rates of abortions in the world — about 5 to 7 abortions per 1,000 women of reproductive age, compared to 18 per 1,000 in the UK, 21 per 1,000 in North America, and an average of approximately 29 per 1,000 women worldwide.

Until the 1960s, the Netherlands was a traditional country with strong family values. Birth control was not discussed and all forms of contraception were socially unacceptable and banned from sale, and it had one of the highest birth rates in Europe.

Then things changed. Dutch people became concerned about the increasing population in their country. A movement began to bring family planning issues into the open and encourage people to talk about them. Doctors started offering family planning services to their patients and sex education was introduced into schools. The ban on contraception was removed and the pill and other modern contraceptives were made available through the national health scheme.

In 1984 the restrictive abortion laws were changed to allow abortion up to 24 weeks (although in practice it is usually 21 weeks). Women do not have to give a reason for an abortion other than the fact that the pregnancy is unwanted. However, they do have to discuss it with their doctor who will make sure that all other options have been fully considered.

If a woman decides to go ahead with an abortion she must wait for five days after first seeing her doctor in order to give herself time to think carefully about her decision. If she goes ahead, the abortion is carried out in a hospital or licensed clinic and is free for women living in the country.

The view of abortion in the Netherlands is that it should be avoided wherever possible. Dutch society as a whole is geared towards preventing unwanted pregnancies, especially among teenagers. As a way of achieving this, schools, public education campaigns, and the media all support a positive attitude of non-judgmental, open discussion on sexual behavior and the responsible use of contraception. It appears to be working.

viewpoints

"...there are international campaigns afoot to reduce birth-rates, sometimes using methods that respect neither the dignity of the woman, nor the right of parents to choose responsibly how many children to have; graver still, these methods often fail to respect even the right to life. The extermination of millions of unborn children, in the name of the fight against poverty, actually constitutes the destruction of the poorest of all human beings."
Pope Benedict XVI, Message for the World Day of Peace, January 2009.

"...reproductive rights embrace certain human rights that are already recognized in national laws, international human rights documents and other consensus documents. These rights rest on the recognition of the basic right of all couples and individuals to decide freely and responsibly the number, spacing and timing of their children and to have the information and means to do so, and the right to attain the highest standard of sexual and reproductive health. It also includes their right to make decisions concerning reproduction free of discrimination, coercion and violence..."
Programme of Action of the International Conference on Population and Development, UN, 1994.

Timeline

1760 BCE One of the earliest known codes of law, the Code of Hammurabi, specifies that a fine must be paid by anyone causing a woman to miscarry.

1550 BCE The Egyptian Ebers Papyrus documents ancient medical knowledge, including descriptions of inducing abortion.

400s BCE The Greek physician Hippocrates advises against the use of drugs to bring about an abortion, but describes other methods.

400s CE St Augustine condemns abortion as a sin but allows that the sin might be less great if it happened before the fetus had a soul.

1025 The Islamic physician Ibn Sina (or Avicenna) describes various substances that can be used for birth control and abortion in his medical encyclopedia.

1200s The Roman Catholic Pope Innocent III declares that abortion before quickening is not murder, but that after quickening it is. For the next 600 years, common law in the UK and elsewhere largely follows the Church's ruling.

1803 A law is passed in the UK making abortion after quickening a crime punishable by death, with a lesser punishment for abortion before quickening.

1820s Laws forbidding abortion appear in most states throughout the US.

1829 New York becomes the first state in the US to specifically allow abortion only on the grounds of saving a mother's life.

1839 Madame Restell (Ann Lohman) starts providing illegal abortions and birth control services in New York.

1850s The first rubber condoms and diaphragms become available.

1861 The Offences Against the Person Act is passed in the UK. This makes abortion at any time and for any reason punishable by imprisonment for anything from 3 years to life.

1873 The Comstock Law makes it illegal to sell, produce, or own information or products to do with birth control and abortion in the US.

1886 Pope Leo XIII forbids any procedure that will directly kill a fetus, even if it is done to save the woman's life. The Catholic Church has maintained this position ever since.

1918 Sale of condoms is legalized in the US.

1920 Abortion is made entirely legal in the Soviet Union.

1932 Poland becomes the first European country to legalize abortion in the case of rape or danger to the mother's health.

1936 The Comstock Law is relaxed in the US, but is not finally removed until 1965.

1938 In the UK, Dr. Alec Bourne is acquitted of the charge of performing an illegal abortion. This case establishes a legal principle for allowing abortion under certain circumstances.

1958 The vacuum aspiration or suction method of abortion is first used in China. It is introduced into the UK in 1967, and eventually to the US and elsewhere.

1960s The contraceptive pill becomes available.

1967 In the UK, the Abortion Act makes abortion legal for medical reasons up to 28 weeks of pregnancy and with the agreement of two doctors.

1973 In the US, the Supreme Court ruling in the *Roe v. Wade* court case establishes for the first time the right of American women to have an abortion within the first trimester.

1970s-1980s France, West Germany, New Zealand, Italy, and the Netherlands legalize abortion under specific circumstances.

1988 The newly invented abortion pill first becomes available in France.

1988 In judging the case of *Morgentaler et al. v. Her Majesty The Queen*, the Supreme Court declares all abortion laws in Canada to be unconstitutional. Canada becomes one of the few countries in the world that has no laws relating to abortion, although there are some state restrictions.

1990 In the UK, the Abortion Act is amended to 24 weeks.

2002 The Australian Capital Territory becomes the first state in Australia to legalize abortion in full and remove all abortion laws. In 2008, the state of Victoria also decriminalises abortion.

2007 Portugal makes abortion fully available up to 10 weeks.

2007 Mexico State becomes the only state in Mexico where abortion is available within the first 12 weeks. In all other states abortion is severely restricted.

2010 Abortion in Spain becomes available on request within the first 12 weeks.

Glossary

Abortifacient A medical drug or substance that is used to bring about an abortion.

Abortion pill A combination of two drugs: mifepristone and misoprostol (prostaglandin) taken to abort a fetus. It is also sometimes known as RU486. The abortion pill should not be confused with the morning-after pill – see below.

Abstinence To hold back or refrain from doing something, especially to avoid having sexual intercourse.

Birth control The methods used to avoid pregnancy, usually by means of contraception.

Conception There is some debate about the precise meaning of this term. It can be said to be either the moment when a female egg cell is fertilized by a male sperm cell, or about a week later, at the moment when a fertilized egg cell implants into the womb.

Condom A thin rubber sheath or covering worn over a man's penis during sexual intercourse to prevent his sperm from entering the woman's vagina.

Constitution A set of principles, customs, or laws formed by a country, state, or organization as a guide to how it should be governed.

Contraception The use of some kind of drug, device, or other technique to avoid the possibility of getting pregnant while having sexual intercourse.

Contraceptive pill A tablet which is taken regularly in order to prevent the production of a female egg cell each month.

Embryo The unborn young of a mammal or other vertebrate animal in the early stages of its development – in human terms in the first eight weeks after the egg cell has implanted.

Fallopian tubes Two tubes leading from a woman's ovaries (where her egg cells are stored) to her womb.

Family planning The entire process of controlling the number of children a couple have and the timing of when they have them, including helping women to become pregnant as well as helping them to avoid it.

Fertilized In human reproduction, a female egg cell is fertilized when it is entered by a male sperm cell. The two cells combine and begin to produce other cells, eventually forming an embryo and then a fetus.

Fetus The unborn young of a mammal or other vertebrate animal while it is still in the womb or egg, and more specifically the name given to a developing human baby in the womb from 8 weeks until birth.

Intrauterine device (IUD) A small plastic or metal contraceptive device placed inside the womb to prevent male sperm cells from reaching a female egg cell.

Midwives Modern midwives are trained nurses who specialize in helping women to give birth. In the past, "midwife" was a term used to describe any women who regularly assisted others during birth, and sometimes helped them to prevent a birth.

Miscarriage The loss of a fertilized egg, embryo, or fetus due to natural causes.

Morning-after pill Also known as emergency contraception. This is a single pill taken as soon as possible after unprotected intercourse in order to prevent an egg from being released and so prevent a possible pregnancy. It is not 100 percent effective and will not work if the woman is already pregnant.

Placenta An organ that develops in the womb after a fertilized egg has implanted there. Its purpose is to pass food and oxygen from the mother's body to the developing fetus and to remove waste products from the fetus.

Pro-choice People and organizations, particularly in the US, who support the right of women to have an abortion describe themselves as being "pro-choice."

Pro-life People and organizations, particularly in the US, who are opposed to abortion describe themselves as being "pro-life."

Sterilization A type of birth control in which a part of the male or female reproductive organs is surgically removed or blocked in order to prevent the production of sperm or egg cells. It does not prevent sexual intercourse.

Trimester A period of time meaning three months.

Viable The point in a fetus' development at which it is thought to be capable of surviving outside the mother's womb.

Womb (or uterus) Part of the female reproductive system and the organ within which a fertilized egg cell develops into an embryo and then a fetus.

Further reading

Armstrong, Nancy and Elizabeth Henderson. *100 Questions You'd Never Ask Your Parents*. Richmond, VA: Uppman Publishing, 2007.

Baumbardner, Jennifer. *Abortion & Life*. New York: Akashic Books, 2008.

Bringle, Jennifer. *Reproductive Rights: Making the Right Choices*. New York: Rosen Publishing, 2010.

Carlson-Berne, Emma. *Introducing Issues with Opposing Viewpoints: Teen Pregnancy*. Farmington Hills, MI: Greenhaven, 2006.

Ehrlich, J. Shoshanna. *Who Decides? The Abortion Rights of Teens*. Westport, CT: Praeger Publishers, 2006.

Greenhouse, Linda and Reva Siegel. *Before Roe v. Wade: Voices That Shaped the Abortion Debate Before the Supreme Court's Ruling*. New York: Kaplan, 2010.

MacKay, Jenny. *Hot Topics: Teen Pregnancy*. San Diego, CA: Lucent, 2011.

Singular, Stephen. *The Wichita Divide: The Murder of Dr. George Tiller and the Battle Over Abortion*. New York: St. Martin's, 2011.

Wicklund, Susan and Alan Kesselheim. *This Common Secret: My Journey as an Abortion Doctor*. New York: PublicAffairs, 2007.

Williams, Heidi. *Issues That Concern You: Teen Pregnancy*. Farmington Hills, MI: Greenhaven, 2009.

Web Sites:

Due to the changing nature of Internet links, Rosen Publishing has developed an online list of Web sites related to the subject of this book. This site is regularly updated. Please use this link to access this list:

http://www.rosenlinks.com/etde/abor

Index